Blackbird

Eleanor Farjeon (1881–196
ant children's writers of the twentieth ...
published over 80 books of poetry, short stories, novels,
plays and autobiography, amongst them *The Little
Bookroom, The Old Nurse's Stocking Basket, Silver-Sand and
Snow* and *A Nursery in the Nineties*. In 1956 she was
awarded the Carnegie and Hans Andersen Medals and
in 1959 the Regina Medal from the United States. The
Eleanor Farjeon Award is presented annually, in her
memory, for outstanding service to Children's Literature.

Anne Harvey has edited over 30 anthologies of Poetry
and Drama and presents literary programmes for
platform performances and radio. In 1992 her antho-
logy *Shades of Green* won the Signal Award for Poetry.
Her work on Eleanor Farjeon includes many articles
and broadcasts, a children's story, *A Present for Nellie*,
and a re-issue of *Edward Thomas: The Last Four Years*.

To the children and staff of
Our Lady of Muswell Catholic Primary School
whose enjoyment of Eleanor Farjeon
has been an inspiration.

ELEANOR FARJEON

Blackbird Has Spoken

Selected Poems for Children

Chosen by
ANNE HARVEY

MACMILLAN
CHILDREN'S BOOKS

First published 1999 by Macmillan Children's Books

This edition published 2000 by Macmillan Children's Books
a division of Macmillan Publishers Limited
25 Eccleston Place, London SW1W 9NF
Basingstoke and Oxford
www.macmillan.co.uk

Associated companies throughout the world

ISBN 0 330 37184 3

1 3 5 7 9 8 6 4 2

A CIP catalogue record for this book is available from
the British Library

Typeset by SX Composing DTP, Rayleigh, Essex
Printed and bound in Great Britain by Mackays of Chatham plc, Kent

Contents

Boys' Names, Girls' Names

School-Bell

Meeting Mary

Introduction

Eleanor Farjeon always wanted to be a writer when she grew up and loved words in poems, stories and songs from her early childhood. In a poem called *English* she wrote:

> As gardens grow with flowers
> English grows with words,
> Words that have secret powers,
> Words that give joy like birds.
>
> Some of the words you say,
> Both in and out of school,
> Are brighter than the day,
> And deeper than a pool.
>
> Some words there are that dance,
> Some words there are that sigh,
> The fool's words come by chance,
> The poet's to heaven fly.
>
> When you are grown, your tongue
> Should give the joys of birds;
> Get while you are young
> The gift of English words.

Her father, B.L. Farjeon was an author and encouraged his children's reading and writing. As a poor boy from an East End family he worked hard to educate himself, and by the time Eleanor and her brothers, Harry, Joe and Herbert were born he had a library of 8,000 books.

"It would have been more natural to live without clothes than without books," wrote Eleanor. "As unnatural not to read as not to eat."

Every Sunday her father gave each child a book to keep and Eleanor, known as Nellie then, treasured these and became a real bookworm. She had poor eyesight and wore thick spectacles, and I think she was like the girl in her poem *Mary Indoors* who said, "Oh, let me be, please let me be, I want to read by the fire."

At 6 came her first complete story, *Kitty's Dream*, in pencilled capital letters and the sort of spelling mistakes all children make. At 7 came the play of *Snow White* and a Valentine poem for a boy called Button. She told him:

> My heart did never beat before
> As it did beat just now;
> I want you but to keep to me
> And I'll give my hand to thou . . .
>
> You've turned away from me just once
> But if you won't again
> I'll give you all the love my heart
> Will ever and can contain.

Her father said he would rather lose a £1 note than lose the special book in which he kept her writing. A £1 note was worth a great deal of money in the 19th Century.

Eleanor Farjeon, was born in 1881 when Queen Victoria was on the throne. She never went to school. A governess taught the four children at home, but they had plenty of time to follow their own interests. Maggie, their pretty, gentle mother, daughter of Joseph Jefferson, a famous American actor, put Harry, the eldest, in charge of the Nursery. He was the inventor of games and events, the maker of rules about fair-play and hand-washing, especially before touching his beloved piano. He decided that bread and butter could only be dipped into tea on Tuesdays and Fridays, and was really strict about bed times. Eleanor was 16 before she broke his 9 p.m. rule, and perhaps the poem *Bedtime* comes from then.

Many ideas come from Eleanor's past, those long-ago days when the Muffin Man's bell was a welcome sound, and Lamplighters lit street lamps at night.

Eleanor was dreamy, imaginative, scared of night darkness, train-tunnels, heights and the waves of the sea. Outside her home she was painfully shy, hating parties where other little girls seemed cleverer and prettier. Best of all she liked going to the theatre and the acting game she and Harry played endlessly, dressing up and becoming the characters in Greek myths, Shakespeare and their favourite books. In time the younger boys were allowed to join in and all four grew wild with excitement until Harry, the leader, brought them down to earth again with:

"We're Harry. . . Nellie . . . Joe and Bertie. We are US again."

When Eleanor was 15 one of her stories so pleased her father that he told her, "I have hopes of you, Nell. I think you're going to make a writer some day.' All her life she never forgot his words.

She published over 80 books for children and adults and had many friends who were writers, among them Edward Thomas, Robert Frost, D.H. Lawrence and Walter de la Mare. Harry became a well known musician, and both Joe and Bertie were popular writers. Sometimes Eleanor and Bertie wrote together. "Collaborators' Honour" was the code for their partnership, meaning, "Neither of us ever tells anyone who wrote what!" I've included some of their joint work in this selection.

I first discovered Eleanor Farjeon's poems when I was at school and we acted out her *Nursery Rhymes of London Town*, clever verses where she turned London place-names upside down giving double meanings to King's Cross, Battersea, Piccadilly and the rest.

Then, in 1981 I made a radio programme about her for her centenary, and met people who had known her. They all praised her bubbling personality, humour, wisdom, and great gift for friendship. Friends and family would flock to the cottage with the blue front door in Hampstead, North London, where there was always a delicious tea (she loved her food!), stories being told, tunes from her musical boxes, her collection of fans to admire . . . and always cats who came for meals and comfort to this woman "whose heart was so big it had room for them all." Cats were her passion, especially golden ones.

In later years she was no longer that shy little Nellie, but rather plump and even more short-sighted, and apt to hug the gas-meter man or the postman by mistake, and once, a friend recalled, to arrive at the Opera wearing one slipper and one plimsoll.

She died in 1965, aged 84, never knowing that her hymn, *Morning Has Broken* became famous world-wide, or that each year there is an *Eleanor Farjeon Award* for Children's Literature presented in her memory. She never really liked personal publicity.

Once when I visited the churchyard where she is buried I found a cat sitting on her grave. I wasn't at all surprised; after all, she herself told us "Cats sleep anywhere."

Anne Harvey
February 1998

It Was Long Ago

It Was Long Ago

I'll tell you, shall I, something I remember?
Something that still means a great deal to me.
It was long ago.

A dusty road in summer I remember,
A mountain and an old house, and a tree
That stood, you know,

Behind the house. An old woman I remember
In a red shawl with a grey cat on her knee
Humming under a tree.

She seemed the oldest thing I can remember,
But then perhaps I was not more than three.
It was long ago.

I dragged on the dusty road, and I remember
How the old woman looked over the fence at me
And seemed to know

How it felt to be three, and called out, I remember,
"Do you like bilberries and cream for tea?"
I went under the tree

And while she hummed, and the cat purred, I remember
How she filled a saucer with berries and cream for me
So long ago,

Such berries and such cream as I remember
I never had seen before, and never see
Today, you know.

And that is almost all I can remember,
The house, the mountain, the grey cat on her knee,
Her red shawl, and the tree,

And the taste of the berries, the feel of the sun I remember,
And the smell of everything that used to be
So long ago,

Till the heat on the road outside again I remember,
And how the long dusty road seemed to have for me
No end, you know.

That is the farthest thing I can remember.
It won't mean much to you. It does to me.
Then I grew up, you see.

Do You Know The Muffin Man?

Do you know the Muffin Man
  Who lives in Drury Lane?
Of course I know the Muffin Man!
  His name is Alfred Payne,
His daughter's name is Mary Ann,
  His wife's is Sarah Jane.

His Mary Ann's a wonder at
  The mixing of a muffin.
She rolls it round, she rolls it flat,
  And puts the best of stuff in,
And if you praise her, sniffs, "Wot, *that?*
  Lor' bless yer, that ain't nuffin'!"

His Sarah Jane's a marvel when
  She's making of a crumpet.
She'll punch it full of holes and then
  Inside the oven dump it,
And snort when it comes out again,
  "Them that don't like can lump it."

Then Alf piles up his green-baize tray
  In snow or shine or rain,
And all round London rings his way
  His livelihood to gain.
Who *doesn't* know the Muffin Man
  That lives in Drury Lane?

Light the Lamps up, Lamplighter!

Light the lamps up, Lamplighter,
    The people are in the street –
        Without a light
        They have no sight,
And where will they plant their feet?
Some will tread in the gutter,
And some in the mud – oh dear!
Light the lamps up, Lamplighter,
Because the night is here.

Light the candles, Grandmother,
    The children are going to bed –
        Without a wick
        They'll stumble and stick,
And where will they lay their head?
Some will lie on the staircase,
And some in the hearth – oh dear!
Light the candles, Grandmother,
Because the night is here.

Light the stars up, Gabriel,
    The cherubs are out to fly –
        If heaven is blind
        How will they find
Their way across the sky?
Some will splash in the Milky Way,
Or bump on the moon – oh dear!
Light the stars up, Gabriel,
Because the night is here.

Bedtime

Five minutes, five minutes more, please!
  Let me stay five minutes more!
Can't I just finish the castle
  I'm building here on the floor?
Can't I just finish the story
  I'm reading here in my book?
Can't I just finish this bead-chain –
  It *almost* is finished, look!
Can't I just finish this game, please?
  When a game's once begun
It's a pity never to find out
  Whether you've lost or won.
Can't I just stay five minutes?
  Well, can't I stay just four?
Three minutes, then? two minutes?
  Can't I stay *one* minute more?

The Night Will Never Stay

The night will never stay,
The night will still go by,
Though with a million stars
You pin it to the sky;
Though you bind it with the blowing wind
And buckle it with the moon,
The night will slip away
Like sorrow or a tune.

The Sounds in the Evening

The sounds in the evening
Go all through the house,
The click of the clock
And the pick of the mouse,
The footsteps of people
Upon the top floor,
The skirts of my mother
That brush by my door,
The crick in the boards,
And the creak of the chairs,
The fluttering murmurs
Outside on the stairs,
The ring at the bell,
The arrival of guests,
The laugh of my father
At one of his jests,
The clashing of dishes
As dinner goes in,
The babble of voices
That distance makes thin,
The mewings of cats
That seem just by my ear,
The hooting of owls
That can never seem near,
The queer little noises
That no one explains –
Till the moon through the slats
Of my window-blind rains,
And the world of my eyes
And my ears melts like steam
As I find in my pillow
The world of my dream.

Waking Up

Oh! I have just had such a lovely dream!
And then I woke,
And all the dream went out like kettle-steam,
Or chimney-smoke.

My dream was all about – how funny, though!
I've only just
Dreamed it, and now it has begun to blow
Away like dust.

In it I went – no! in my dream I had –
No, that's not it!
I can't remember, oh, it is *too* bad,
My dream a bit.

But I saw something beautiful, I'm sure –
Then someone spoke,
And then I didn't see it any more,
Because I woke.

The Tide in the River

The tide in the river,
The tide in the river,
The tide in the river runs deep.
I saw a shiver
Pass over the river
As the tide turned in its sleep.

Night-Piece

Now independent, beautiful, and proud,
Out of the vanishing body of a cloud
Like its arisen soul the full moon swims
Over the sea, into whose distant brims
Has flowed the last of the light. I am alone.
Even the diving gannet now is flown
From these unpeopled sands. A mist lies cold
Upon the muffled boundaries of the world.
The lovely earth whose silence is so deep
Is folded up in night, but not in sleep.

*Evening hushes
The thoughts of the poplars,
The dreams of the rushes.*

Oh, Hark!

Oh, hark, my darling, hark!
I hear the owl in the dark,
The white, low-flying owl
Along the air doth prowl
    With her strange, lonely wail.

And hark, my darling, hark!
I hear the stars in the dark,
I hear the singing sky
Shaking with melody! –
    It is the nightingale.

Once Upon a Time

Once Upon a Time

Once Upon a Time,
Once Upon a Time!
Everything that happened, happened
Once Upon a Time!

Lovely ladies wed with beasts,
Tablecloths provided feasts
        When addressed in rhyme
Magic fish could not refuse
Anything you cared to choose,
Kitchenmaids wore crystal shoes,
        Once Upon a Time!

Little girls in scarlet hoods
Talked with wolves and things in woods,
        Bullfrogs in the slime
Lived enchanted in their fen
Till Kings' Daughters stooped again,
Kissed, and changed them into men,
        Once Upon a Time!

Once Upon a Time,
Once Upon a Time!
Younger Sons were in their glory,
And the end of every story
        Was a wedding chime;
Girls made ladders of their tresses,
Magic nuts held fairy dresses,
Princes wed the right Princesses,
        Once Upon a Time!

What has happened? Nothing happens!
   Life is past its prime,
Everything that happened, happened
   Once Upon a Time.

C is for Charms

I met a Strange Woman
With things in her arms.
"What have you got, Woman?"
"Charms," she said, "charms.

"I will put one on you
Ere I have done.
Which shall I put on you?"
"None," I said, "none!"

Oh how she smiled at me.
"Nay, then, my dear,
Look, do but look at them.
What do you fear?

"I've a black charm of night
And a gold one for noon,
A white charm for winter,
A rose charm for June;

"I've a green charm for woods,
And a blue charm for water,
And a silver for moons
When they're in their first quarter.

"I've a slow charm for growth,
And a swift one for birds,
And a soft one for sleep,
And a sweet one for words.

"I've a long charm of love,
And a strong charm for youth,
And one you can't change
Or destroy, for the truth.

"Sorry's the man, my dear,
Sorry,"she said,
"Who wanders through life
With no charm on his head."

Oh how she smiled at me.
"Big one or small,
Which shall I put on you?"
"All," I said, "all!"

J is for Jinn

If ever in a foreign land
You're going to meet a Jinn,
Keep a bottle close at hand
For to put him in.

You cannot slay him with a sword,
A blow would go right through him,
You cannot bind him with a cord
Because there's nothing to him.

So since you cannot shoot him, or
Garrotte him by the throttle,
Just keep a bottle by you, for
He can't resist the bottle.

When the last bit of him has gone
Inside it, seal it neatly
With the Great Seal of Solomon,
Which does for Jinns completely.

Q is for Quince

The Quince tree has a silken flower,
 The Quince tree has a downy fruit,
The Quince tree is a curious bower
 Of greeny leaves and gnarly root.
Its shape is like a witch grown old,
 Its flowers like fairies, and it bears
Quinces that when their down turns gold
 Look still more beautiful than pears.
And oh, whoever smells the Quince
 Knows that the fairies must have placed
The scent there – *but don't taste it, since*
 It was the Witch who made the taste!

Toad-Flax

Toad, toad, old toad,
    What are you spinning?
Seven hanks of yellow flax
    Into snow-white linen.
What will you do with it
    Then, toad, pray?
Make shifts for seven brides
    Against their wedding-day.
Suppose e'er a one of them
    Refuses to be wed?
Then she shall not see the jewel
    I wear in my head.

The Witch! The Witch! Don't let her get you!
Or your Aunt wouldn't know you the next time she met you.

W is for Witch

I met a wizened woman
As I walked on the heath,
She had an old black bonnet
Her small eyes peeped beneath,
Her garments were so shabby
She couldn't have been rich,
She hobbled with a crutchstick,
And I knew she was a Witch.

She peered at me so slyly
It made my heart feel queer,
She mumbled as she passed me,
But what I couldn't hear.
I smiled at her for answer
And wished her a good day,
She nodded and she chuckled
And she hobbled on her way.

And so I got home safely.
I didn't drop the eggs,
My nose had grown no longer,
My legs were still my legs,
I didn't lose my penny
Or tumble in a ditch –
So mind you smile and say "Good day,"
When *you* meet a Witch.

Tippetty Witchet

Tippetty Witchet
Lived by a wood
In a blue pinafore
And a green hood;
Her hut was of wattle,
Her bed was of wool,
Her fire was of fir cones,
Her bath was a pool.

She plaited sweet rushes
For shoes for her feet,
She bound birchen besoms
To keep her floor neat,
She picked fallen acorns
To roast for her tea,
And one of her picking
She set for a tree.

Tippetty Witchet
Died so long ago
That no one remembers
She ever was so;
Her wattles are scattered,
Her bed's trod in mire,
Her pool wants for water,
Her hearth has no fire.

But rich with tall timber,
And dark with broad shade,
Are fifty green acres
Round Tippetty's glade;
And old bones get brushwood
That's better than food,
And young bones get acorns
In Tippetty's wood.

And what does it matter
If nobody knows
Who gave the old these things,
And gave the young those,
Who wore a blue pinafore
And a green poke,
And planted the acorn
That turned into oak?

Pegasus

From the blood of Medusa
Pegasus sprang.
His hoof upon heaven
Like melody rang,
His whinny was sweeter
Than Orpheus' lyre,
The wing on his shoulder
Was brighter than fire.

His tail was a fountain,
His nostrils were caves,
His mane and his forelock
Were musical waves,
He neighed like a trumpet,
He cooed like a dove,
He was stronger than terror
And swifter than love.

He could not be captured,
He could not be bought,
His running was rhythm,
His standing was thought;
With one eye on sorrow
And one eye on mirth,
He galloped in heaven
And gambolled on earth.

And only the poet
With wings to his brain
Can mount him and ride him
Without any rein,
The stallion of heaven,
The steed of the skies,
The horse of the singer
Who sings as he flies.

Argus and Ulysses

Argus was a puppy,
Frisking full of joy.
Ulysses was his master,
Who sailed away to Troy.

Argus on the sea-shore
Watched the ship's white track,
And barked a little puppy-bark
To bring his master back.

Argus was an old dog,
Too grey and tired for tears,
He lay outside the house-door
And watched for twenty years.

When twenty years were ended
Ulysses came from Troy.
Argus wagged an old dog's wag,
And then he died for joy.

Don't go looking for fairies,
   They'll fly away if you do.
You never can see the fairies
   Till they come looking for you.

Nearly

Into the room
I crept so soft –
I scarcely breathed,
And I never coughed –
So soft, they could hardly
Know I was there,
Into the room
With oh, such care
I crept – that I *nearly*
Broke their Law,
They were just in time,
But I *nearly* Saw!

Out in the dark
I stood so still –
Like a bit of the door
Or the window-sill –
So still, they could hardly
Think of me,
Out in the dark
So noiselessly
I stood – that I *nearly*
Got the Word,
They were just in time,
But I *nearly* Heard!

Down in the wood
I tried so hard,
Hoping to get them
Off their guard,
So hard, they could scarcely
Get away,
Down in the wood
So *hard* that day
I tried – that I *nearly*
Got right through,
They were just in time,
But I *nearly* knew!

Coach

There was a yellow pumpkin
Born on a pumpkin-patch,
As clumsy as a 'potamus,
As coarse as cottage-thatch.
It longed to be a gooseberry,
A greengage, or a grape,
It longed to give another scent
And have another shape.
The roses looked askance at it,
The lilies looked away –
"This thing is neither fruit nor flower!"
Their glances seemed to say.

One shiny night of midsummer,
When even fairies poach,
A good one waved her wand and said,
"Oh Pumpkin! be a coach!"
A coach of gold! a coach of glass!
A coach with satin lined!
If you could seek a thousand years,
Such you would not find.
The Princess in her crystal shoes
Eager for the dance
Stepped inside the pumpkin-coach
And rolled to her romance.

The roses reached out after it,
The lilies looked its way –
"Oh that we were pumpkins too!"
Their glances seemed to say.

I Sent a Letter to my Love

She wrote him a letter,
She wrote to her love,
She slipped her wee love-letter
Under her glove.

It had seventeen darlings,
And thirty-one dears,
And fifty-nine kisses,
And one or two tears.

She went to the pillar-box
Meaning to post it,
But when she arrived there,
Good gracious! she'd lost it!

And someone or other,
But who she can't prove,
Has picked up the letter
She wrote to her love.

If the butcher or baker
Or milkman or sweep
Has laughed at her letter
For shame she will weep.

Suppose all those darlings
And dears go amiss?
Suppose someone's stolen
A tear or a kiss?

It's as cruel as caging
A soft-breasted dove
To keep back the letter
She wrote to her love.

Satin

I had a satin slipper,
A single satin slipper
My mother left behind her
      The day she danced away.
So I stood on one toe,
Had to stand on one toe,
With t'other toe behind me
      I just danced away.

I met the Lord of London,
The lofty Lord of London.
Before he fell behind me
      He knelt in my way.
"One-foot-in-air-miss,
What about a pair, miss?
Cast a look behind you
      Before you dance away."

I paired with him in satin,
Sheeny-shiny satin,
Seven yards behind me
      The train trailed away,
And my one satin slipper,
Glossy as a kipper.
I've never looked behind me
      From that day.

Until I can earn me a shilling a year,
I'll go in silk, because satin is dear.

Tailor

I saw a little Tailor sitting stitch, stitch, stitching
Cross-legged on the floor of his kitch, kitch, kitchen.
His thumbs and his fingers were so nim, nim, nimble
With his wax and his scissors and his thim, thim, thimble.

His silk and his cotton he was thread, thread, threading
For a gown and a coat for a wed, wed, wedding,
His needle flew as swift as a swal, swal, swallow,
And his spools and his reels had to fol, fol, follow.

He hummed as he worked a merry dit, dit, ditty:
"The Bride is as plump as she's pret, pret, pretty,
I wouldn't have her taller or short, short, shorter,
She can laugh like the falling of wat, wat, water,

"She can put a cherry-pie, togeth, geth, gether,
She can dance as light as a feath, feath, feather,
She can sing as sweet as a fid, fid, fiddle,
And she's only twenty inches round the mid, mid, middle."

The happy little Tailor went on stitch, stitch, stitching
The black and the white in his kitch, kitch, kitchen.
He will wear the black one, she will wear the white one,
And the knot the Parson ties will be a tight, tight, tight one.

Cotton

My wedding-gown's cotton,
　　My wedding-gown's cheap,
It's crisper than sea-foam
　　And whiter than sheep,
Printed with daisies
　　In yellow and green,
A prettier wedding-gown
　　Never was seen!
Light-heart and light-foot
　　I'll walk into church
As straight and as slim
　　As a silvery birch,
And after my wedding
　　I never will lay
Like ladies my wedding-gown
　　Lightly away.
I'll wash it in soapsuds
　　As fresh as when new,
And rinse it in rainwater
　　Softer than dew,
And peg it on Saturdays
　　High on the line,
And wear it on Sundays
　　Full of sunshine.
My wedding-gown's cotton,
　　It cost me a crown,
Was ever girl wed in
　　A commoner gown? –
As birds in the branches,
　　As flowers on the green,
The commonest wedding-gown
　　Ever was seen!

Wheelbarrow

He dumped her in the wheelbarrow
    And trundled her away!
How he chaffed and how she laughed
    On their wedding-day!

He bumped her through the garden-gate,
    He bounced her down the lane!
Then he reeled and then she squealed,
    And off they bounced again.

He jiggled her across the ditch,
    He joggled her through the holt!
He stubbed his toe and she cried O!
    Whenever she got a jolt.

He wiggled her up the bridle-path,
    He woggled her through the street –
Down he stumbled! down she tumbled,
    Right at the Parson's feet!

The Mother's Tale

Just before bed,
"Oh, *one* more story,
Mother!" they said,
And in the glory
Of red and gold
Beyond the fender
Their Mother told
Splendour on splendour.

A small boy threw
A handful of seeds,
And a beanstalk grew
Faster than weeds
As high as heaven . . .
She wore a red hood . . .
Once there were seven
Dwarfs in a wood . . .

So the children found
A gingerbread house . . .
So Puss with a bound
Killed the Giant-mouse.
"Now, Mother, tell a
Best tale of all!"
So Cinderella
Went to the ball . . .

"Don't stop, Mother!"
It's time to rest.
"Oh, tell us another
The *very* best!"
So the best of all
She told to them:
"Once in a stall
In Bethlehem". . .

Boys' Names, Girls' Names

Boys' Names

What splendid names for boys there are!
There's Carol like a rolling car,
And Martin like a flying bird,
And Adam like the Lord's First Word,
And Raymond like the Harvest Moon,
And Peter like a piper's tune,
And Alan like the flowing on
Of water. And there's John, like John.

Girls' Names

What lovely names for girls there are!
There's Stella like the Evening Star,
And Sylvia like a rustling tree,
And Lola like a melody,
And Flora like a flowery morn,
And Sheila like a field of corn,
And Melusina like the moan
Of water. And there's Joan, like Joan.

Fie, fie!
Rockaby!
Babes must sleep, they must not cry.

The Mother Sings

Rockaby, my baby,
Slumber if you can.
I wonder what you're going to be
When you're grown a man.

If you are a monarch
On a gold and silver throne,
With all the lands of East and West
For to call your own,
I know you'll be the greatest monarch
Ever was known.

If you are a poet
With the magic of the word,
A swan's quill to write with
And a voice like a bird,
I know you'll be the greatest poet
Ever was heard.

But whether you're a monarch
And make your bride a queen,
Or whether you're a poet
With men's hearts to glean,
I know you are the sweetest baby
Ever was seen.
Rockaby, my baby,
Slumber if you can.
I wonder what you're going to be
When you're grown a man.

Treasure

What have you picked up, baby, on the shore?
Such treasure as was never found before!
    A pebble white as snow
    And one as round as O!
    A curly, yellow shell,
    One flat and pink as well;
    A crab, a tinier thing
    Than daddy's signet-ring;
    A bit of glass so blue
    The sky cannot look through;
    And seaweed green as cress,
    And soft as mother's tress.

Carry them home and strew them on the floor –
Tomorrow you can run and get some more.

Jill Came from the Fair

Jill came from the Fair
With her pennies all spent.
She had had her full share
Of delight and content;
She had ridden the ring
To a wonderful tune,
She had flown in a swing
Half as high as the moon,
In a boat that was drawn
By an ivory swan
Beside a green lawn
On a lake she had gone,
She had bought a gold packet
That held her desire,
She had touched the red jacket
Of one who ate fire,
She had stood at the butt,
And although she was small
She had won a rough nut
With the throw of a ball,
And across the broad back
Of a donkey a-straddle,
She had jolted like Jack-
In-the-Box on a saddle –
Till 'mid frolic and shout
And tinsel and litter,
The lights started out
Making everything glitter,
And dazed by the noise
And the blare and the flare,
With her toys and her joys
Jill came from the Fair.

Sue Went to the Fair

Sue went to the Fair
With sixpence to spend –
And when she got there
It had come to an end!
The stall that sold sweets
And the tent that sold toys
Were cleared of their treats
For small girls and boys!
The big switchback stand
Was a skeleton hill,
The round-about band
Had grown silent; and still
As pictures the wagons,
The boats, and queer breeds
Of emus and dragons
And gold-saddled steeds;
The coconut sticks
Without heads stood about,
Like tall candle-wicks
Whose lights were blown out;
The shooting-booth had
Not a single bright prize
For the skilful young lad
Who could hit the bulls' eyes:
The tall spiral tower
Had fallen asleep,
And sent down no shower
Of folk in a heap;
And the motionless herds
Of red and blue swings
Hung listless as birds
That are clipped in their wings.

Oh where was the glitter
The Fair should reveal?
The grass was a litter
Of paper and peel,
The tent-ropes were slackened,
The flares were unlit,
The fairway was blackened
With cinders and grit!
And the men with brown arms,
And the girls with black hair
Who had packed up the charms
And the toys of the Fair,
Had no smiles for Sue.
She had come as their friend
But nobody knew
She had sixpence to spend.

Fred

Fred likes creatures,
And has a lot of them.
Bees don't sting him,
He's got a pot of them,
Little round velvety bodies they are
Making honey in Fred's jam-jar.

Fred likes creatures.
Hedgehogs don't prickle him,
They flatten their quills
And scarcely tickle him,
But lie with their pointed snouts on his palm,
And their beady eyes are perfectly calm.

Fred likes creatures.
The nestling fallen out
Of the tree-top
With magpie calling out
Where? where? where? contented lingers
In the round nest of Fred's thick fingers.

Fred likes creatures.
Nothing's queer to him,
Ferrets, tortoises,
Newts are dear to him.
The lost wild rabbit comes to his hand
As to a burrow in friendly land.

Fred *eats* rabbit
Like any glutton, too,
Fred eats chicken
And beef and mutton too.
Moral? None. No more to be said
Than Fred likes creatures, and creatures like Fred.

For a Boy in a Plum-Tree

Freddy, Freddy,
Up in the Plum!
Greedy, Greedy,
Throw me down some!
If you throw me down Stones and don't throw me Plums,
I shan't sing out when the Gardener comes.

Minnie

Minnie can't make her mind up,
Minnie can't make up her mind!
    They ask her at tea,
     "Well, what shall it be?"
    And Minnie says, "Oh,
    Muffins, please! no,
    Sandwiches – yes,
    Please, egg-and-cress –
    I mean a jam one,
    Or is there a ham one,
Or is there another kind?
    Never mind!
             Cake
    Is what I will take,
The sort with the citron-rind,
    Or p'r'aps the iced one –
    Or is there a spiced one,
Or is there the currant kind?"
    When tea is done
    She hasn't begun,
She's always the one behind,
Because she can't make her mind up,
Minnie *can't* make up her mind!

I simply can't tell you how glad I am
When the Marmalade is Apricot Jam!

David

Yes, David puts his toys away,
And washes behind his ears,
    If he climbs a tree
    And scrapes his knee
He doesn't resort to tears;
He never gives girls and boys away,
He has the politest tones,
In fact, he is a *good* little boy,
But he *will – throw – stones*.

He throws them at the window-panes,
He throws them at the water,
He throws them at his Aunty Jane's
Inoffensive daughter,
He throws them for old Rover to
Bring back again like treasure,
He throws them Over, At, and Through,
For nothing else but pleasure;
He shies at acorns, conkers, cones,
And always scores a single,
He chucks his stones at other stones
Lying on the shingle,
He aims at stumps and sitting hens,
He marks down running rabbits –
It's just another of you men's
Incalculable habits.
He has no motive deep and dark,
That isn't it a bit, it
Is: that when David spies his mark
He *simply – has* – to hit it.

David gives his things away,
And brushes his teeth at night,
    He seldom fails
    To clean his nails,
And get his homework right,
And everybody brings away
The same report with groans:
"David is a good little boy,
But he *does – throw – stones*!"

Julia, John, and Jane

Julia, John, and Jane
Went for a walk in the rain.

Julia said, "Oh dear, oh dear!
I'll get my best frock wet, I fear,
And my nice new shoes will be covered with dirt,
And my nice clean gloves will take some hurt,
And my hat will lose its fancy shape –
Why didn't I bring my mackintosh cape?"
Julia's one to complain
When she goes for a walk in the rain.

John said, "Golly! what fun!
I'll take off my boots and run
In the wettest grass that my feet can find!
I'm soaked before and I'm soaked behind,
But *I* don't care how wet I get,
It's jolly good sport to get thoroughly wet!" –
John is as happy again
When he goes for a walk in the rain.

And what about Jane?

Jane was thinking, "I wonder
How you'd keep an air-balloon under
The sea, if you happened to get it there?
I wonder if ever a William pear
Could grow on a pearmain apple-tree?
I wonder what people had for tea
Before there was any tea at all?
And why a ball wouldn't *be* a ball
If it was square instead of round?

I wonder what happens to a sound
After I've said it? I wonder why – "

Julia said, "Come into the dry
Under this tree
Out of the rain!"
But John only said, "Not me!"
And Jane,
When she heard Julia start complaining,
Wondered, "I wonder *why* it's raining?"

Jenny White and Johnny Black

Jenny White and Johnny Black
Went out for a walk.
Jenny found wild strawberries,
And John a lump of chalk.

Jenny White and Johnny Black
Clambered up the hill.
Jenny heard a willow-wren,
And John a workman's drill.

Jenny White and Johnny Black
Wandered by the dyke.
Jenny smelt the meadow-sweet,
And John a motor-bike.

Jenny White and Johnny Black
Turned into the lane.
Jenny saw the moon by day,
And Johnny saw a train.

Jenny White and Johnny Black
Walked into a storm.
Each felt for the other's hand
And found it nice and warm.

Myfanwy Among the Leaves

Dying leaf and dead leaf,
Yellow leaf and red leaf
And white-backed beam,
Lay long the woodland road
As quiet as a dream.

Summer was over,
The year had lost her lover,
Spent with her grief
All along the woodland road
Leaf fell on leaf.

Then came a shuffling,
Such a happy ruffling
Of the dried sweet
Surf of leaves upon the road
Round a baby's feet.

Year-old leaf ran after
Three-year-old laughter,
Danced through the air
As she caught them from the road
And flung them anywhere.

Old leaf and cold leaf,
Brown leaf and gold leaf
And white-backed beam,
Followed down the woodland road
Myfanwy in a dream.

School-Bell

School-Bell

Nine-o'clock Bell!
Nine-o'clock Bell!
All the small children and big ones as well,
Pulling their stockings up, snatching their hats,
Cheeking and grumbling and giving back-chats,
Laughing and quarrelling, dropping their things,
These at a snail's pace and those upon wings,
Lagging behind a bit, running ahead,
Waiting at corners for lights to turn red,
Some of them scurrying,
Others not worrying,
Carelessly trudging or anxiously hurrying,
All through the streets they are coming pell-mell
At the Nine-o'clock
Nine-o'clock
Nine-o'clock
Bell!

Books

What worlds of wonder are our books!
As one opens them and looks,
New ideas and people rise
In our fancies and our eyes.

The room we sit in melts away,
And we find ourselves at play
With someone who, before the end,
May become our chosen friend.

Or we sail along the page
To some other land or age.
Here's our body in the chair,
But our mind is over *there*.

Each book is a magic box
Which with a touch a child unlocks.
In between their outside covers
Books hold all things for their lovers.

French

Isn't it strange
That in Paris
You are Vous
And Moi is Me
And No and Yes
Are Non and Oui!

Isn't it odd
That in Bordeaux
Bread is Pain
And Water Eau
And Good and Fair
Are Bon and Beau!

Isn't it queer
That in Calais
French *isn't* French
And *is* Français!
What sort of French
Can that be, pray?

Latin

When Julius Caesar was a child
In Rome, the same things drove him wild
        As now in England fidget us.
He blubbered in the Latin tongue:
"*Mater*, a naughty *Apis* stung
        Me here, upon the *Digitus!*"
(By which he meant: "A naughty Bee
Has stung my finger, Mother, see!")

His *Mater* took him on her knees,
And cooed: "Those horrid little Bees!
        Now why did Jove invent 'em?"
And then she calmed her *Filius*
And put upon his *Digitus*
        A soothing *Unguentum.*
(Which means, she smeared an Ointment on
The finger of her little son.)

At tea, to make her Julius well,
She gave him *Panis*, spread with *Mel* –
        (And if you think that's funny,
It only means *your* Mother might
Console you for an insect-bite
        At tea with Bread-and-Honey).
Now, Honey's such a pleasant thing
He quite forgot his *Apis* sting.

Though Julius Caesar lived in Rome,
And you inside a British home,
    You're very like that brat in
The things he said when he was young,
Though you speak in the English tongue,
    And Julius spoke in Latin.
So when you say a Latin word,
That is the one which Caesar heard.

History

All down the ages
Like a great tide,
Commoners walking
Where noblemen ride,
Now in the sunshine
And now in the shade,
People move onward
While History's made.

Churchmen make churches
And Lawyers make codes,
Builders make cities
And Romans make roads,
Soldiers make battles,
And Merchants make trade,
And people make changes
While History's made.

Craftsmen and Artists
Make manifold things,
Rulers make nations,
And nations make kings –
All down the ages
In great cavalcade,
People move onward,
And History's made.

The King's Cake

King Alfred he could sing a song
    As sweet as any man's:
King Alfred he could fight a throng,
    And think out battle-plans:
King Alfred from his heart so true
    The English Laws could make:
But one thing Alfred couldn't do –
    He couldn't bake a cake.

I'd rather be like Alfred than
    Like any other King;
I'd rather, more than any man,
    Hear Alfred play and sing:
I'd rather keep, for England's sake,
    The laws he made for me –
But I'd rather eat my Mother's cake
    Than Alfred's for my tea.

Robin Hood
14th Century

Robin Hood
Was an outlawed earl
He took to the wood
With a lovely girl,
And there and then
They were lord and queen
Of a band of men
In Lincoln green –
There was Scarlet Will, and Alan a Dale,
And great big Little John-O,
And Friar Tuck, that fat old buck,
And much the Miller's son-O!

Robin Hood
He robbed the rich
And gave to the good
And needy, which,
When the moon was bright
And the sport was rare,
Seemed only right
And fair and square
To Scarlet Will, and Alan a Dale,
And great big Little John-O,
And Friar Tuck, that fat old buck,
And Much the Miller's son-O!

Robin Hood
He poached the deer
And moistened his food
With stolen beer –
Hark how they sing
And shout and flout
The knavish king
Who turned him out
With Scarlet Will, and Alan a Dale,
And great big Little John-O,
And Friar Tuck, that fat old buck,
And Much the Miller's son-O!

Joan of Arc
1412 – 1431

Maid, what make you
Among your sheep?
Over the meadows,
As in sleep,
I hear the Voices,
Brighter than wine,
Of Margaret, Michael,
Catherine!

Maid, what make you
Of their tale?
Doff your kirtle,
Don your mail,
And save fair France,
Say the divine
Margaret, Michael,
Catherine!

Maid, what make you
At Orleans siege?
I force the English
I free my liege,
I crown my king,
And obey the sign
Of Margaret, Michael,
Catherine!

Maid, what make you
In Rouen Town?
I feel a flame!
I wear a crown!
Father in Heaven,
I see them shine,
Margaret, Michael,
Catherine!

Henry VIII
1509

Bluff King Hal was full of beans;
He married half a dozen queens;
For three called Kate they cried the banns,
And one called Jane, and a couple of Annes.

The first he asked to share his reign
Was Kate of Aragon, straight from Spain –
But when his love for her was spent,
He got a divorce, and out she went.

Anne Boleyn was his second wife;
He swore to cherish her all his life –
But seeing a third he wished instead,
He chopped off poor Anne Boleyn's head.

He married the next afternoon
Jane Seymour, which was rather soon –
But after one year as his bride
She crept into her bed and died.

Anne of Cleves was Number Four;
Her portrait thrilled him to the core –
But when he met her face to face
Another royal divorce took place.

Catherine Howard, Number Five,
Billed and cooed to keep alive –
But one day Henry felt depressed;
The executioner did the rest.

Sixth and last came Catherine Parr,
Sixth and last and luckiest far –
For this time it was Henry who
Hopped the twig, and a good job too.

Elizabeth I
1558

Hail, Queen Elizabeth! Here comes Queen Bess
In a very big ruff and a very wide dress;
Her hair it is red, and her eyes they are green,
And England has prospered since Bess became Queen.

The boldest of sailors have sailed to the West,
The greatest of poets have written their best,
The gayest of people have danced on the green,
And England's grown merry since Bess became Queen.

She's vain as a peacock that opens its tail,
She's proud as an eagle that weathers the gale,
She's crafty and jealous, suspicious and mean,
But England *is* England now Bess is the Queen.

Pocahontas
1595 – 1617

Pocahontas
Gentle and wild,
The Indian Chief
Powhatan's child,
In her deerskin-shoes
And her feather-cloak
Lived in Virginia
With her folk.

The red-leaf'd maple,
The pine-tree strong,
The wild-bee's honey,
The oriole's song,
The arrow's whistle,
The victim's yell,
Pocahontas
Knew these things well.

But when the White Men
Sought her land,
These she did not
Understand;
They came like heroes
Of ancient myth,
And when she saw him
She loved John Smith.

The Indian called
The White Man foe,
But Pocahontas
Did not so;

From the tomahawk
And the scalping-knife
Powhatan's daughter
Saved John Smith's life.

For when her idol
Was doomed to die
And bowed his head
As the blade rose high,
Her own brown body
On his she flung
And death was stayed
As the axe-head swung.

And did she wed
The man she saved?
Her story was not
So engraved.
John Rolfe, the settler,
Made her his bride,
And brought her to England,
Where she died.

But Pocahontas
In memory runs,
Under Virginia's
Moons and suns,
Swift and eager,
Gentle and wild,
The Indian Chief
Powhatan's child.

Emmeline Pankhurst
1858 – 1928

Militant, vigorous,
Rampant and rigorous,
Emmeline Pankhurst cried, "Britain! take note!
Vote, Votes for Women! I
Won't rest, by Jiminy,
Till, like my husband, I'm given a Vote!
Are men superior?
Women inferior?
Suffragettes, come! pass your days and your nights
Hatching up critical
Crisis political,
Fearlessly planned to procure us our Rights!"

Then with her following,
Hooting and hollowing,
Emmeline shouted when Ministers spoke;
Windows they battered in;
Acid they scattered in
Pillar-posts, setting the letters a-smoke;
Next, from the putting-green
They started cutting green
Pieces of turf twice as big as your hand –
Thus her tenacity,
Backed by audacity,
Made Mrs Pankhurst the scorn of the land.

Statesmen detested her,
Policemen arrested her,
Colonels in clubs became pink at her name,
Newspapers sneered at her,
Little boys jeered at her,
Still Mrs Pankhurst went on with the game,
Till her ability
Vanquished hostility –
Now women vote, for a vote they have got –
And since her victory,
No contradictory
Candidate dares to suggest they should not!

Poetry

What is Poetry? Who knows?
Not the rose, but the scent of the rose;
Not the sky, but the light in the sky;
Not the fly, but the gleam of the fly;
Not the sea, but the sound of the sea;
Not myself, but what makes me
See, hear, and feel something that prose
Cannot; and what it is, who knows?

The Gate in the Wall

The Gate in the Wall

The blue gate in the wall,
The small blue gate is gone,
And I alone
Know all
That was once seen beyond this thick
Barrier of new brick.
There was a paved walk, long
And narrow,
Where the small throng
Of saxifrages green
Crept in between
The cracks; there was a barrow
Half full of withered flowers;
A pear tree, and a bush of silver broom;
And in that open room,
When there were sunny hours,
A graceful lady walked,
With hair as snowy as the pear-tree bloom,
And voice that always talked
As from a little distance. She
Was gone before the blue gate went from me.

But I shall see
Often through this new brick
What other eyes will not be quick
Enough to see:
The lady who once moved
Tending the beds and borders that she loved,
Whose work was never done,
Now in the early morning, now the late
Warm afternoon, but always touched with sun,
Wandering in the air
Of other summers, through the small blue gate
That is no longer there.

March, You Old Blusterer

March, you old blusterer,
    What will you bring?
Sunny days, stormy days,
    Under your wing?
No matter which it be,
    You will bring spring.

Whether Lion roaring comes
    Over bleak hills,
Whether Lamb bleating goes
    Seeking sweet rills,
You will bring primroses
    And daffodils.

Whether the earth shows a
    White or green quilt,
Where in both hedge and tree
    Men hear a lilt,
March, you old blusterer,
    Nests will be built.

How many daisies can you count on your lawn?
When you can count twelve daisies, spring has come.

A Morning Song
For the First Day of Spring

Morning has broken
Like the first morning,
Blackbird has spoken
  Like the first bird.
Praise for the singing!
Praise for the morning!
Praise for them, springing
  From the first Word.

Sweet the rain's new fall
Sunlit from heaven,
Like the first dewfall
  In the first hour.
Praise for the sweetness
Of the wet garden,
Sprung in completeness
  From the first shower.

Mine is the sunlight!
Mine is the morning
Born of the one light
  Eden saw play.
Praise with elation,
Praise every morning
Spring's re-creation
  Of the First Day!

Keep Still

Look, and keep very still,
Still as a tree,
And if you do you will
Presently see
The doe come down to drink
Leading her fawn
Just as they did, I think,
In the first dawn.

Hark, not a sound, my dear,
Be quiet and hark,
And very soon you'll hear
The vixen bark,
And see her cubs at play
As I believe
They played in starlight grey
On the first eve.

Look, and keep very still.
Hark, not a sound!
The pretty creatures will
Soon be around,
At play and drink, as though
They drank and played,
Cub, vixen, fawn and doe,
Ere men were made.

Pancake Tuesday

Run to Church with a Frying-Pan!
A Kiss for the Woman, a Cake for the Man.

Run to Church with a frying-pan,
    Never you lose a minute!
Run to Church with a frying-pan
    And a yellow pancake in it.

First to carry her pancake there,
    Though heavy or light she beat it,
Must toss her cake to the Bellringer,
    And the Bellringer must eat it.
Then be she madam or be she miss
    All breathless after rushing,
The Bellringer shall give her his kiss
    And never mind her blushing.

Run to Church with a Frying-Pan!

A Kiss for the Woman, a Cake for the Man —

A Dragon-Fly

When the heat of the summer
Made drowsy the land,
A dragon-fly came
And sat on my hand,
With its blue jointed body,
And wings like spun glass,
It lit on my fingers
As though they were grass.

There are Big Waves

There are big waves and little waves,
Green waves and blue.
Waves you can jump over,
Waves you dive through,
Waves that rise up
Like a great water wall,
Waves that swell softly
And don't break at all,
Waves that can whisper,
Waves that can roar,
And tiny waves that run at you
Running on the shore.

Sand

The Sand is the Sand, till you take it
    And make it
Whatever you fancy – just see
    What things Sand can be!
A castle, a fortress, a wall,
    A tunnel, a ball,
A hole, or a boat, or a seat,
    Or a pudding to eat,
A garden, a churchyard, a hill –
    Sand is just what you will,
Until you've gone home to your tea,
    And the incoming sea
Washes out all the labours you planned again.
    Then, Sand is Sand again.

K is for King of the Castle

I am the King of the Castle
    (Get down, you Dirty Rascal!)
I am the King of the Castle,
    And here I mean to stand
Until the sea has found me
And come up all around me,
On every side to bound me
    And cut me off from land.

I've built the highest Castle
(Get *down*, you Dirty Rascal!)
The highest and finest Castle
    Of all upon the sand,
With moats and bridges and towers,
A garden of shells, and bowers
Of seaweed trees and flowers,
    And here I take my stand.

And when I hear the mothers
Calling to all the others,
I will not go with my brothers
    Back to the dusty land;
For I'm the King of the Castle,
I *am* the King of the Castle,
I am the *King* of the Castle,
    And here I mean to stand!

The Waves of the Sea

Don't you go too near the sea,
  The sea is sure to wet you.
Harmless though she seems to be
  The sea's ninth wave will get you!
But I can see the small white waves
  That want to play with me –
They won't do more than wet my feet
  When I go near the sea.

Don't you go too near the sea,
  She does not love a stranger,
Eight untroubled waves has she,
  The ninth is full of danger!
But I can see the smooth blue waves
  That want to play with me –
They won't do more than wet my knees
  When I go near the sea.

Don't you go too near the sea,
  She'll set her waves upon you.
Eight will treat you playfully,
  Until the ninth has won you.
But I can see the big green waves
  That want to play with me –
They won't do more than wet my waist
  When I go near the sea.

Don't you go too near the sea,
    Her ways are full of wonder.
Her first eight waves will leave you free,
    Her ninth will take you under!
But I can see the great grey waves
    That want to play with me –
They won't do more than wet my neck
    When I go near the sea.

Don't you go too near the sea –
    O Child, you set me quaking!
Eight have passed you silently,
    And now the ninth is breaking!
I see a wave as high as a wall
    That wants to play with me –
O Mother, O Mother, it's taken me all,
    For I went too near the sea!

Poppies

Cold reigns the summer, and grey falls the day,
The flame of the year is smouldering away,
But here in the hedgerow and yonder in the wheat
The flame of the poppy is throwing out its heat.

Small grows the corn and scant is the yield
Of the hay lying strewn upon the stubble field,
And there in the meadow and here by the road
The red poppy glows as in other years it glowed.

Sunrise comes chilly and sunset comes wet,
And low burns the flame where the sun rose and set,
But red as the flame of a dawn that will not pass
The fire of the poppy is lighted in the grass.

Pencil and Paint

Winter has a pencil
For pictures clear and neat,
She traces the black tree-tops
Upon a snowy sheet.
But autumn has a palette
And a painting-brush instead,
And daubs the leaves for pleasure
With yellow, brown, and red.

Now! Says Time

NOW! Says Time,
and lifts his finger,
and the leaf on the lime
may not linger.
When Time utters
NOW! and lifts
his finger, the oakleaf flutters
and drifts,
and elm and beech
let a leaf fall from the bough
when, finger lifted, to each
Time says NOW!

Down, down!
Yellow and brown
The leaves are falling over the town.

"Punkie-Night"
(A Somersetshire Custom on 30 October)

Here come children
On Punkie-night
With mangold-lanterns,
And candle-light
Gleaming inside
The goblin-faces'
Yellowy grins
And gold grimaces.
In and out
Of Hinton St George,
By church and hostel,
By farm and forge,
Swinging their gargoyle
Mangolds bright,
There go children
On Punkie-night.

Hallowe'en

On Hallowe'en the old ghosts come
About us, and they speak to some;
To others they are dumb.

They haunt the hearts that loved them best;
In some they are by grief possessed,
In other hearts they rest.

They have a knowledge they would tell;
To some of us it is a knell,
To some a miracle.

They come unseen and go unseen;
And some will never know they've been,
And some know all they mean.

The Bonfire

This cloud of smoke in other hours
Was leaves and grass, green twigs and flowers.

This bitter-sweet dead smell that blows
Was once the breathing of the rose.

Shapeless the forms of petals fair
And slender leaves melt on the air,

And in a scent she never knew
In life, the rose departeth too.

Burning the Gate

We're burning up the old blue garden gate,
The little gate as old as dead Queen Anne,
That stood between the small ground and the great,
The gardens of the master and the man.

After two centuries the blue gate stumbled
Betwixt its posts, and hung and swung askew,
The slats were worm-eaten, the paint was crumbled,
And it must be replaced by something new.

The angry hand that pushed it is forgotten,
The tender, hesitating hand about
Its latch was dust before the latch was rotten –
Now even those old touches are burned out.

 Yes, now the flame is turning it to ash,
 All goings and all comings by its way
 Are smoking up the chimney, and a flash
 Of fire wipes out two centuries in a day.

To an Oak Dropping Acorns

With my two arms I cannot span thy girth,
Yet when I pick thy acorn from the earth
Within my hand I hold a ship at sea,
My bed, my table, and my own roof-tree.

Silver-Sand and Snow

Here's the soft snow again,
    See now, once more,
Drifts at the window-pane,
    Drifts by the door.

Run for your wooden spade,
    Which it may be
Silver-sand castles made,
    Drowned by the sea.

Build now your tower here;
    Let it be done
Ere it shall disappear
    Drowned by the sun.

All our best castles and
    Towers end so,
Builders in silver-sand,
    Dreamers in snow!

Snow

Oh the falling Snow!
        Oh the falling Snow!
Where does it all come from
Whither does it go?
Never never laughing,
Never never weeping,
Falling in its Sleep,
Forever ever sleeping –
From what Sleep of Heaven
Does it flow, and go
Into what Sleep of Earth
The falling falling Snow?

Carol of the Signs

Whiter than silver shines
Last night's fallen snow,
It is thick with signs,
Yet I saw none go.

Naked feet, three pair,
Left prints upon the snow,
Because the feet were bare,
Poor men's feet, I know.

Wheels of chariots rolled
Last night across the snow,
Great men in the cold
Rode before cockcrow.

Lo! a newborn lamb
Ran on the fallen snow,
By his side his dam
Gently trod and slow.

Here a Cross was laid
Heavy on the snow,
Somebody here stayed
To rest a moment so.

And here, the brightest scar
Of all upon the snow,
The imprint of a Star,
A heavenly Star, dropped low.

Thick as dew on grass
Lie signs upon the snow,
Yet I heard none pass,
And I saw none go.

The Song of the Fir

There was a fir
Within a wood,
Far away, far away:
It stands no longer where it stood.
Dance around the tree today.

It had a scent
Made sweet the air,
Far away, far away:
The sweetness is no longer there.
Breathe the sweetness as you play,
And dance around the tree today.

It grew between
The earth and sky,
Far away, far away:
The tree has lost its liberty
And between four walls must stay.
Breathe the sweetness as you play,
And dance around the tree today.

On its tip
It bore a cone,
Far away, far away:
Now that simple fruit is gone
Hang the tree with presents gay
Mid the walls where it must stay,
Shedding sweetness where you play,
And dance around the tree today.

In the Week When Christmas Comes

This is the week when Christmas comes,
    Let every pudding burst with plums,
And every tree bear dolls and drums,
    In the week when Christmas comes.

Let every hall have boughs of green,
With berries glowing in between,
    In the week when Christmas comes.

Let every doorstep have a song
Sounding the dark street along,
    In the week when Christmas comes.

Let every steeple ring a bell
With a joyful tale to tell,
    In the week when Christmas comes.

Let every night put forth a star
To show us where the heavens are,
    In the week when Christmas comes.

Let every pen enfold a lamb
Sleeping warm beside its dam,
    In the week when Christmas comes.

This is the week when Christmas comes.

Christmas Stocking

What will go into the Christmas Stocking
While the clock on the mantelpiece goes tick-tocking?
    An orange, a penny,
    Some sweets, not too many,
    A trumpet, a dolly,
    A sprig of red holly,
    A book and a top
    And a grocery shop,
    Some beads in a box,
    An ass and an ox
    And a lamb, plain and good,
    All whittled in wood,
    A white sugar dove,
    A handful of love,
    Another of fun,
    And it's very near done –
    A big silver star
    On top – there you are!
Come morning you'll wake to the clock's tick-tocking,
And that's what you'll find in the Christmas Stocking.

Meeting Mary

Meeting Mary

Hard by the Wildbrooks I met Mary,
When berries smelled sweet and hot.
Mary, I fancy, was seven years old,
And I am never mind what.

"What are you getting?" I asked Mary.
"Blackberries. What are you?"
"Toadflax," I answered Mary, "and mushrooms."
"How many mushrooms?" "Two."

"Going to have blackberries stewed for dinner,
Or blackberry jam?" said I.
"Not goin' to have neither," said Mary;
"Goin' to have blackberry pie."

"Aren't you lucky!" I said Mary.
"And what sort of name have you got?"
"*My* name's Mary," said Mary, "what's *your* name?"
I told her never mind what.

"Goodbye, Mary." "Goodbye," said Mary,
And went on picking and eating.
That's all about my meeting with Mary –
It's my favourite sort of meeting.

Mary Indoors

Aren't you coming out, Mary?
      Come out: your eyes will tire –
Oh, let me be, please, please, said she,
      I want to read by the fire.

What are you reading, Mary,
      That keeps you, keeps you in? –
Oh, wonderful things of knights and kings
      With their heart's desire to win.

Look out of window, Mary!
      The blustering day is bright.
Come fight the wind with us, and find
      The sun on the hilly height.

Come on out of it, Mary,
      And win your heart's desire! –
Oh, let me be, please, *please*, said she,
      I want to read by the fire.

For Mary and her Kitten

The Kitten's in the Dairy!
Where's our Mary?
She isn't in the Kitchen,
She isn't at her Stitching,
She isn't at the Weeding,
The Brewing, or the Kneading!
Mary's in the Garden, walking in a Dream,
Mary's got her Fancies, and the Kitten's got the Cream.

A Kitten

He's nothing much but fur
And two round eyes of blue,
He has a giant purr
And a midget mew.

He darts and pats the air,
He starts and pricks his ear,
When there is nothing there
For him to see and hear.

He runs around in rings,
But why we cannot tell;
With sideways leaps he springs
At things invisible –

Then half-way through a leap
His startled eyeballs close
And he drops off to sleep
With one paw on his nose.

Cats

Cats sleep
Anywhere,
Any table,
Any chair,
Top of piano
Window-ledge,
In the middle,
On the edge,
Open drawer,
Empty shoe,
Anybody's
Lap will do,
Fitted in a
Cardboard box,
In the cupboard
With your frocks –
Anywhere!
They don't care!
Cats sleep
Anywhere.

Mr Sheraton's Cat *

Mr Sheraton had a cat,
I'm certain of that.

Mr Sheraton's cat's
Pats
Posed so prettily on the floor –
Two behind and two before,
While puss herself demurely stood
Graceful, proportioned, perfect, good –
That Mr Sheraton, eyeing the sweet
Turn of those small fastidious feet,
Cried: "Eureka! at last I'm able
To turn the legs of my chair and table!"
Men praised his work, then and thereafter.

The feline race subdues its laughter,
And gazing down its exquisite legs
To its turned-out pads that can walk on eggs,
Purrs: "Mr Sheraton's credit? *That's*
Mr Sheraton's cat's."

* Thomas Sheraton (1751-1806) was the last of the great English
cabinet-makers of the eighteenth century.

To Coney: My Kitten
(A Poem Under Difficulties)

Kitten like a ball of gold,
Not much more than ten weeks old,
Must you really try to bite
My penholder as I write?
Must you really cut up capers
All among my notes and papers?
Must you really do you think
Dip your tail into my ink,
And on my tale wipe it dry?
Do you really have to try
Making a duet of it
While I type-write, golden kit?
Kitten! that's my pencil, please!
Kitten! these are my two knees!
Kitten! why, by all the laws,
Have you pins instead of claws?
Kitten! I am not a tree –
Don't come clambering up me!
Go away, you little blighter!
You're a kitten, I'm a writer,
And, if you my verses chew,
How can I buy milk for you?
Did you hear me – Go away! . . .

Oh, all right, then. Stay and play.

The Golden Cat

My golden cat had dappled sides;
No prince has worn so fine a cloak,
Patterned like sea–water where rides
The sun, or like the flower in oak
When the rough plank has been planed out,
Lovely as yellow mackerel skies
In moonlight, or a speckled trout.
Clear as swung honey were his eyes.

It was a wondrous daily thing
To look for, when his beautiful
Curved body gathered for a spring
That, light as any golden gull,
Flashed over the fine net of wire
Which my casement-window bars;
His leap was bright as tongues of fire,
And swift as autumn shooting-stars.

My cat was like a golden gift,
A golden myth of Grecian lore –
But things so bright, and things so swift
Must vanish; and he is no more.

Cat!

Cat!
Scat!
Atter her, atter her,
Sleeky flatterer,
Spitfire chatterer,
Scatter her, scatter her
       Off her mat!
       Wuff!
       Wuff!
       Treat her rough!
Git her, git her,
Whiskery spitter!
Catch her, catch her,
Green-eyed scratcher!
       Slathery
       Slithery
       Hisser,
       Don't miss her!
Run till you're dithery,
       Hithery
       Thithery!
       Pfitts! pfitts!
       How she spits!
       Spitch! spatch!
       Can't she scratch!

Scritching the bark
Of the sycamore-tree,
She's reached her ark
And's hissing at me
   Pfitts! pfitts!
   Wuff! wuff!
    Scat,
    Cat!
    That's
    That!

Bliss

Let me fetch sticks,
Let me fetch stones,
Throw me your bones,
Teach me your tricks.

When you go ride,
Let me go run
You in the sun,
Me at your side;

When you go swim,
Let me go too
Both lost in blue
Up to the brim;

Let me do this,
Let me do that –
What you are at,
That is my bliss.

Outside

He's pulling on his boots!
He's going out again –
Out to the world of roots,
The whipping wind and rain,
The stinging sun that tells
On bristles and in blood,
Out to the place of smells,
And things that move, and mud;
Out where, to run a race,
Is not to hit a wall;
Out to the time of chase!
Will he whistle and call?
He's looking for his stick,
He's – Hark! his glorious shout!
I'm coming quick-quick-quick!
We're going out! We're *Out*.

Inside

A bellyful and the fire,
And him in his old suit,
And me with my heart's desire,
My head across his foot.

And I doze. And he reads.
And the clock ticks slow.
And, though he never heeds,
He knows, and I know.

Presently, without look,
His hand will feel to tug
My ear, his eyes on book,
Mine upon the rug.

Epitaph

What is this Stone he's laid upon my bones
For whom I fetched and carried endless stones?
Wait, Master, wait a little. When we meet
You'll know me by my Stone, laid at your feet.

Invitation to a Mouse

There's pudding in the pantry,
  There's jam upon the shelf,
There's bacon in a pastry pie
  On a dish of delf –
Mousiekin, wee Mousiekin,
  Go and help yourself!
But please, Mousie, please,
Don't touch the toasted cheese,
For if you do mayhap
Something will go snap!
And the pudding and the jam
And the pastry and the ham
Will have to stay untasted, all wasted on the shelf.

The White Blackbirds

Among the stripped and sooty twigs of the wild-cherry tree
Sometimes they flit and swing as though two blossoms of the
    Spring
Had quickened on these bleak October branches suddenly.

They are like fairy birds flown down from skies which no
    one knows,
Their pointed yellow bills are bright as April daffodils,
Their plumy whiteness heavenly as January snows.

Loveliest guests that choose our garden-plot for loitering!
Oh, what a sudden flower of joy is set upon the hour
When in their cherry cages two white blackbirds sit and
    swing.

Kestrel

Still hangs the Kestrel there
High in the still air
When the day is fair.

So still he seems to stay
He might in the fair day
Be fixed there far away.

But presently he will
Swoop from his airy hill
And make some small bird still.

The Birds of Joy
Shall nest in my hair,
The Birds of Sorrow
Shall not rest there.
O Bird of Sorrow,
Take to wing!
Bird of Joy,
O sit and sing!

Kingfisher

A flicker of blue
Under the sallows –
Over the shallows
A Kingfisher flew!

St Francis' Day*

Come forth, O beasts! This is the day
        Of that dear Saint who called you brother,
Who greeted you upon the way
        As one companion does another,
And saw in God's creative plan
No difference between beast and man.

Fly down, O birds! This is the day
        Of that sweet Saint who sister named you,
Who, coming in your midst to pray,
        By love, and by love only, tamed you,
And read in the Creator's word
Equal delight for man and bird.

What! not one furry thing runs out?
        What! not a single flying feather?
Men separate with fear and doubt
        What love was wont to bring together.
To bird and beast we call in vain
Till Brother Francis walks again.

* St Francis' Day is October 4th.

Mrs Malone

Mrs Malone
Lived hard by a wood
All on her lonesome
As nobody should.
With her crust on a plate
And her pot on the coal
And none but herself
To converse with, poor soul.
In a shawl and a hood
She got sticks out-o'-door,
On a bit of old sacking
She slept on the floor,
And nobody, nobody
Asked how she fared
Or knew how she managed,
For nobody cared.
    Why make a pother
    About an old crone?
    What for should they bother
    With Mrs Malone?

One Monday in winter
With snow on the ground
So thick that a footstep
Fell without sound,
She heard a faint frostbitten
Peck on the pane
And went to the window
To listen again.
There sat a cock-sparrow
Bedraggled and weak,
With half-open eyelid

And ice on his beak.
She threw up the sash
And she took the bird in,
And mumbled and fumbled it
Under her chin.
 "Ye're all of a smother,
 Ye're fair overblown!
 I've room fer another,"
 Said Mrs Malone.

Come Tuesday while eating
Her dry morning slice
With the sparrow a-picking
("Ain't company nice!")
She heard on her doorpost
A curious scratch,
And there was a cat
With its claw on the latch.
It was hungry and thirsty
And thin as a lath,
It mewed and it mowed
On the slithery path.
She threw the door open
And warmed up some pap,
And huddled and cuddled it
In her old lap.
 "There, there, little brother,
 Ye poor skin-an'-bone,
 There's room fer another,"
 Said Mrs Malone.

Come Wednesday while all of them
Crouched on the mat
With a crumb for the sparrow,

A sip for the cat,
There was wailing and whining
Outside in the wood,
And there sat a vixen
With six of her brood.
She was haggard and ragged
And worn to a shred,
And her half-dozen babies
Were only half-fed,
But Mrs Malone, crying
"My! ain't they sweet!"
Happed them and lapped them
And gave them to eat.
        "You warm yerself, mother,
        Ye're cold as a stone!
        There's room fer another,"
        Said Mrs Malone.

Come Thursday a donkey
Stepped in off the road
With sores on his withers
From bearing a load.
Come Friday when icicles
Pierced the white air
Down from the mountainside
Lumbered a bear.
For each she had something,
If little, to give –
"Lord knows, the poor critters
Must all of 'em live."
She gave them her sacking,
Her hood and her shawl,
Her loaf and her teapot –
She gave them her all.

"What with one thing and t'other
Me fambily's grown,
And there's room fer another,"
Said Mrs Malone.

Come Saturday evening
When time was to sup
Mrs Malone
Had forgot to sit up.
The cat said *meeow*,
And the sparrow said *peep*,
The vixen, *she's sleeping*,
The bear, *let her sleep*.
On the back of the donkey
They bore her away,
Through trees and up mountains
Beyond night and day,
Till come Sunday morning
They brought her in state
Through the last cloudbank
As far as the Gate.
  "Who is it," asked Peter,
  "You have with you there?"
  And donkey and sparrow,
  Cat, vixen and bear

Exclaimed, "Do you tell us
Up here she's unknown?
It's our mother, God bless us!
It's Mrs Malone
Whose havings were few
And whose holding was small
And whose heart was so big
It had room for us all."

Then Mrs Malone
Of a sudden awoke,
She rubbed her two eyeballs
And anxiously spoke:
"Where am I, to goodness,
And what do I see?
My dears, let's turn back,
This ain't no place fer me!"
    But Peter said, "Mother
    Go in to the Throne.
    There's room for another
    One, Mrs Malone."

The Old Man's Toes

Up the street,
Down the street,
My
    Joan
        goes –
(Mind you don't tread upon the
Old
    Man's
        Toes!)
She hops on the pavement
Into every Square,
But she mustn't touch the Cracks in
    between
Them
    There.
The Squares on the pavement
Are safe
        as can
            be:
One is the Sands
By the side
        of the
            sea;
One is a Garden where
Joan's
    flowers
        grow;

One is a Meadow
She
    and I
        know.

But the Cracks are *dangerous,*
As
   Everybody
        knows!
The Cracks in the Pavement are the
Old
   Man's
      Toes.
Anyone who treads on the
Old
   Man's
      Corn
Will wish in a jiffy he had
Never
   been
      born!
For the Sea will roll up and
Suck
   you
      down!
And a horrid blight will turn your
Garden
     brown!
And into the Meadow with an
Angry
   Moo
A Big Cross Cow will come
Rushing
   at
     You!
Up the street and down the street
My
   Joan
     goes –

Here she makes a Pudding,
There she smells a Rose,
Yonder she goes stooping where the
Mushroom
              grows –
(Mind, Joan! don't tread upon the
Old
      Man's
              Toes!)

Roadmender

Where the buses and cabs are so thick
    That they've cracked the poor road into two,
The Roadmender comes with his pick
    To patch up the damage they do.

He ropes off a bit of the street,
    The bit that amuses him best,
And then he has something to eat,
    And leans on his spade for a rest.

He takes up a square block of wood,
    And pauses his forehead to wipe,
And then has a bite more of food,
    And then takes a pull at his pipe.

He looks at the hole he has made
    And thoughtfully scratches his head,
And, stacking his pick and his spade,
    Goes home to his supper and bed.

The Lights at Night

No sooner does the sky grow dark
Than all the town breaks out in lights,
Blue and green and crimson spark
Making a thousand startling sights.

The theatres and advertisements
Dazzle the night with brilliant signs,
And high in air the world's events
Are writ in running golden lines.

The fiery pictures glow and fade,
Clusters of stars wink in and out,
The floodlights pour their bright cascade
From domes and towers round about.

It is as though a magic spell
Had brought to life a fairy town –
Oh, what a jewelled citadel
Is London when the dark comes down!

Battersea

Little Boy, little boy, what is the matter? –
Madam, the sea has been turned into batter!

Little boy, little boy, what does it matter? –
Madam, I cannot go swimming in batter.

Little boy, little boy, that's no great matter! –
Madam, how *shall* I get rid of the batter?

Why, with your spoon and your fork and your platter, see,
Little boy, little boy, eat up the Batter-Sea!

Hammersmith

Hammer, Smith! hammer, Smith!
What will you shoe my pony with?
        I'll shoe it with a shoe of steel,
        Another of gold so red,
        A third shoe of ivory,
        And a fourth shoe of lead.
Then I'll pay with a brass farthing
I picked up out of the roadway,
So hammer, Smith! hammer, Smith!
For I want to ride down the Broadway.

Glasshouse Street

Don't throw stones in Glasshouse Street,
    in Glasshouse Street,
    in Glasshouse Street,
Don't throw stones in Glasshouse Street,
    Or you'll be beat!

Two small boys in Glasshouse Street
One March morning happened to meet –
    A stone flashed,
    A window smashed,
    A chimney-pot crashed,
    And the boys were thrashed!

So don't throw stones in
    Glasshouse Street,
    in Glasshouse Street,
    in Glasshouse Street,
Don't throw stones in Glasshouse Street,
    Whoever you meet!

King's Cross

King's Cross!
                What shall we do?
His Purple Robe
Is rent in two!
Out of his Crown
He's torn the gems!
He's thrown his Sceptre
                Into the Thames!
                The court is shaking
                In its shoe –
                King's Cross!
                What shall we do?
                Leave him alone
                For a minute or two.

For Shadows

When shadows from the East are long,
Then Larks go up for Morning-Song.
When shadows are not seen at all,
Then Green-Leaves into Silence fall.
When Shadows From the West grow long,
Then Blackbirds meet for Evensong.

Index of First Lines

Glitter When You Jump

Poems celebrating the Seven Ages of Woman
Chosen by Fiona Waters

I Have Lived and I Have Loved

I have lived and I have loved;
I have walked and I have slept;
I have sung and I have danced;
I have smiled and I have wept;
I have won and wasted
    treasure;
I have had my fill of pleasure;
And all these things were
    weariness,
And some of them were dreariness.
And all of these things – but
    two things
Were emptiness and pain:
And Love – it was the best of them;
And Sleep – worth all the rest
    of them.

ANON

Charles Causley
Selected Poems for Children

*"Among the English Poetry of the last half century, Charles
Causley's could well turn out to be the best loved and most
needed"*

Dream Poem

I have not seen this house before
Yet room for room I know it well:
A thudding clock upon the stair,
A mirror slanted on the wall.

A round-pane giving on the park.
Above the hearth a painted scene
Of winter huntsmen and the pack.
A table set with fruit and wine.

Here is a childhood book, long lost.
I turn its wasted pages through:
Every word I read shut fast
In a far tongue I do not know.

Out of a thinness in the air
I hear the turning of a key
And once again I turn to see
The one who will be standing there.

Golden Apples
Chosen by Fiona Waters

In this treasure chest of verse, there are poems old and new.
Some are funny, some are sad, but they're all a joy to read.
You'll want to keep this book forever.

Polar Bear

The secret of the polar bear
Is that he wears long underwear.

GAIL KREDENSER

Disturbed, the Cat

Disturbed, the cat
Lifts its belly
On to its back.

KARAI SENRYU

A selected list of poetry books available from Macmillan

The prices shown below are correct at the time of going to press. However, Macmillan Publishers reserve the right to show new retail prices on covers which may differ from those previously advertised.

Another Day on Your Foot and I Would Have Died   0 330 34048 4
Agard, Cope, McGough, Mitchell & Patten   £3.99

Selected Poems for Children   0 330 35404 3
Charles Causley   £5.99

A Spell of Words   0 330 35422 1
Elizabeth Jennings   £4.99

Glitter When You Jump   0 330 34104 9
Edited by Fiona Waters   £3.99

Golden Apples   0 330 29728 7
Chosen by Fiona Waters   £3.99

Five Finger Piglets   0 330 391 305
Duffy, Kay, McGough, Owen & Patten   £3.99

All Macmillan titles can be ordered at your local bookshop
or are available by post from:

Book Service by Post
PO Box 29, Douglas, Isle of Man IM99 1BQ

Credit cards accepted. For details:
Telephone: 01624 675137
Fax: 01624 670923
E-mail: bookshop@enterprise.net

Free postage and packing in the UK.
Overseas customers: add £1 per book (paperback)
and £3 per book (hardback).